D1123039

THE FUNNY SIDE OF

Nursing

STEVENSON PUBLICATIONS LIMITED

This book is published to help raise funds
for COMIC RELIEF and a donation of
10% will be made from every copy sold.

First published 1996

ISBN 0 9526395 2 1

Printed in Great Britain by
D. Brown & Sons Ltd, Bridgend.

Published by
Stevenson Publications Limited
19 Wharfdale Road, London N1 9SB.

INTRODUCTION
By Martin Clunes

A district nurse always came away from one of her leg ulcer patients with a half pound bag of beautifully peeled brazil nuts which she would eat while finishing her rounds. She knew that the patient's son always brought them in but her toothless state made it impossible for her to get through them.

One day the nurse noticed a big box of chocolate covered brazils by the patient's chair and her mouth began to water - that would make a nice change, she thought - but strangely they weren't mentioned and she left empty handed.

The next time she called however, the patient presented her with the usual offering and the nurse felt a bit miffed. "Did you manage the chocolate ones then, dear?" she asked. "Oh no," came the reply, "they're what my son always brings but I haven't the heart to tell him I can only suck the chocolate off."

A keen sense of humour is essential to any nurse and it's a credit to the nursing profession in general that so many are prepared to make fun of themselves.

The stories that follow are told by nurses, doctors, registrars, porters, ambulance men and even the odd consultant (his story appears near the back of the book).

Thanks are due to all those who have contributed material and to you, for forking out the cash to buy this book and, by doing so, contributing to Comic Relief.

3

THE FUNNY SIDE OF NURSING

Soon after I learned the proper technique for a bed bath, I was assigned to my first real patient. The elderly gentleman was sleeping and badly in need of a bath.

I carefully assembled the appropriate equipment, and cautiously wrapped the washcloth, as instructed, to avoid dripping water on the patient. With total concentration, I began to wash him.

I was down to his feet when my tutor entered the room. He looked closely at the patient, then asked me how the bath was going. I replied that the bath was going just fine. He then asked if the patient had moved or made any noise during the procedure. I told him that the patient was quiet and seemed to be enjoying his bath.

He took me out into the hall and explained that the patient I was bathing had expired several hours ago.

A tutor was marking papers late one night and one student's evaluation of her teaching plan jolted her to alertness:
'My patient learned to ambulate to the bathroom, bend at the knees and eat himself.'

One woman, waiting for the results of her blood test, announced that the doctor was checking her little "white morsels."

Another, trying to remember the name of her condition, knew only that it started with an 'n'. Then she suddenly announced: "I'm nemic."

A male patient stated that he had got a bone stuck in his throat because he had not masturbated his food properly.

The patient was brought to the ward in a wheelchair with the porter.

The patient got out of bed while the nurses stripped.

The patient died peacefully, free from pressure sores and in one piece.

The fluid chart is for everything the lady does.

She, as an alcoholic, could share her views and problems with other people on the ward, rather than bottle them up.

Mr Boyle talked to the group on dental hygiene.

The man was sometimes violet towards her.

Since her walking had improved dramatically, steps were taken to get her back to school...this was done for a trail period.

The nursing staff will discuss the patients sleeping with the night staff.

Nurse will chart the patients weight on Mondays wearing daytime clothes without shoes after breakfast.

Physiotherapists can keep the members active...

Initially, because of his large moist size, it was a problem fitting his trousers...

I arranged his trousers, but still his shit was hanging out.

I felt a member of the ward team.

After a whirlwind romance, they were married at a small registry office...she admits their marriage to be a stormy one.

His mother had to rear him up on her own.

She is continent and opens her bowls three times weekly.

A bed cradle was put in situ to take the weight off his legs and cause considerable pain.

After a while the patient was reduced to 2 crutches, 2 walking sticks and 1 stick.

The patient arrived on the ward after a 5 hour ambulance journey at lunch time.

His shopping was done using his car, in the supermarket.

The patient was taught how to use his call system and radio his bed.

She was written up for Ponstan, on her medication chart which had to be taken orally.

In London, if you call for an ambulance, by law one has to go regardless of the type or nature of the call. Many are given to the crew as either 'collapse' or 'please investigate' so they have little or no idea what they will find when they arrive on the scene.

Here are a small selection of some of the more unusual calls received by one ambulance station in less than one year.

1. Forty year old male who has a gum infection. He's had it for eighteen days and it hurts every day at 5pm.

2. Male with eyelash in eye.

3. Twenty seven year old male with shampoo in eye.

4. Thirty year old male has got a rash after a curry.

5. Sneezed whilst on toilet, now has backache.

6. Mother won't let son into house.

7. Twenty nine year old female feels dizzy after getting off a roundabout.

8. Young male was in a car accident three weeks ago and now has pain in his hand.

9. Twenty two year old female not eating, now losing weight.

10. A lady who has had diarrhoea for two years, wants to go to hospital for a second opinion (at 1am).

"I'll finish dessert on the way."

11. Seventeen year old male who's had head and stomach pains for one day. On arrival he was eating scrambled egg and wouldn't leave until he'd finished.

12. Thirty year old female who has had a pain in her knee for twenty five days.

13. Took one tablet four years ago, now body looks disfigured in the mirror.

14. Male had face slapped.

15. Thirty one year old male has been to the dentist twice this week and every time he goes to the toilet he gets a burning pain in his testicles and back passage.

16. A male who has felt weak for over a year.

17. Male with toilet paper stuck up nose.

18. Twenty five year old female has drunk too much now feels sick.

19. Green liquid coming out of nose when he blows it.

20. Young male has had pain in one of his shoulders for three days, now he can't put his arm over his head.

21. "I was bitten by a dog three weeks ago."

22. A male who has a toothache wants the crew to take him to a cash point first so that he can get some money.

23. Twenty five stone male wants crew to wipe his bottom, because he cannot reach.

24. Female wants crew to bring a doctor to her house because she hasn't got time to wait around at the hospital.

25. Fifteen year old female can't get her earring out.

26. Female saw a mouse in her house. She wants crew to catch it.

27. Fourteen year old male keeps breaking out in yellow heads.

28. My legs are all sweaty.

29. I've had bad wind for two days now.

30. I've just eaten fish and chips, I'm allergic to fish.

A wife became concerned about her overworked husband and took him to their physician for a check up. The nurse led them to the examination room and took the husband's vital signs. She then took the wife aside and whispered,
"I don't like the way your husband looks."
"I don't either," said the wife, "but he's always been a good father to the children."

A woman complained that she had been experiencing constant flatus. "Fortunately," she added, "they don't stink."
The physician did his physical exam, then instructed the woman, "Take two of these pills tonight and call me in the morning."
The woman did as he instructed.
In the morning, she discovered that her flatus continued, but now the odour was horrendous. She called him back.
"Well," the doctor replied, "now that I've cured your sinus problem, I'll see what I can do about your flatus."

A nurse went in to check her patient in the ICU who was wearing nasal prongs. The nurse tried to talk to him, but all she could get out of him was gasping and unintelligible talk. Finally, the nurse thrust a note pad and pencil at the patient and said, "I can't hear you Mr X, can you write down what you want?"
The patient weakly scribbled on the pad, *'Get your foot off my oxygen tube!'*

From lecture notes...

There are vast areas to look at in human sexuality.

Prior to the Barium Enema the doctor may need a rectal washout.

Carrying heavy objects can cause bilingual hernias.

Some illnesses are inherited...others seem to run in families.

The patient's mood should be recorded, then passed on to staff.

Sexuality is the in-thing at the moment.

(Referring to effects of the media on drinking habits)
People are drawn more to drink if it is pumped into them nearly 24-hours a day.

"Hey, beautiful! Can I buy you a drink?"

In order to encourage her to care for her personal hygiene, I would wink and tell her I was available whenever she needed a bath.

The patient may be clamped off if she has been using the catheter since her operation.

Strict hourly toileting should be stuck to by the nurse.

On commencement of treatment, the patient will be taken into the treatment room on a bed accompanied by someone who is familiar.

(Referring to client's mouth ulcer)
'It may be due to ill-fitting gums or bad teeth.'

(Nurses report on depressed patient)
She stated to myself and other members of staff on several occasions that she wanted to go to the riverbank and as she sank lower, she began to express suicidal thoughts.

The assessment technique used on the ward initially consists of an objectionable client assessment.

She is a very cooperative lady, keen to articulate her feels.

One important verbal indication is a warning from the patient herself that she is beginning to feel aggressive, which should be encouraged by staff.

No member of staff could successfully reduce her suicidal thoughts. She continued to express them until I left the ward.

If you only have a group of educationalist or clinicians trying to plan the Advances in Psychiatry course, you're going to find yourself in a straight-jacket.

She bought a house with her husband.

With his improvement in gait, he bowed to my request.

She would be able to take her nightie off over her head, but needed assistance to take her arms out.

The girl is 12 years old, just about to start her adolescent period.

I rushed down to the bus-stop which I only just caught.

Student stories...

Following the final exam several of us students sat on the grass and discussed the exam questions. As I left, I heard some of the maintenance workers talking.
"I ain't never going to a hospital again!" said the first.
"Why do you say that?"
"I heard them nurses talking about their test. One said it was 75% guess work and they all agreed!"

As a student nurse , I wanted to dazzle the staff with my comprehension of medical terminology and my ability to decipher barely legible physician's orders. When they had been unable to decipher a recently scribbled order, I cheerfully offered my interpretation.
"Apply vaginal cream to the uvula," I stated proudly.
To the amusement of the staff, a nearby doctor replied,
"Well, if you've managed to reach all the way to the uvula, I think you've applied a bit too much."

An elderly man was admitted to a nursing home by his family, due to his weakening condition. The next morning, the nurse saw him leaning to the extreme left in his chair, so she propped a pillow under that side. Later, she noticed him leaning to the right, so she put a pillow there, too. Soon he was leaning forward, so out came the vest restraint.
His family came to see him, and the nurse explained her efforts to keep him from hurting himself. The family asked the gentleman how he was doing.
"The food is good, the nurse is real nice, but she does her best to stop you from farting in here."

Observations...

The patient should wash his own top half, including his genitals at the side of his bed.

The patient should be encouraged to mobilise little and often to prevent periods of standing when in bed.

Before catheters come out, the bladder should be taught control.

Constipation is a problem that the nurse must keep an eye on.

The patient should be given 500mls a day to drink, plus yesterday's output.

Nurse will assist the patient by letting him lean on an old nurse whilst getting in and out of the bath.

Death only occurs in very fatal cases.

Over the next three days, his leg became more painful and returned to the doctors.

The patient suffers from constipation due to laxative abuse by her mother.

The physiotherapist is informed so that she can come and clap the patient's lungs.

Her husband was allocated to the tea shop while the doctor saw her in out-patients.

I found the staff nurse to be god, and talked good English.

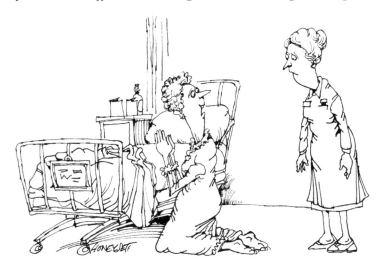

"I'm just having a word with the staff nurse."

The following pages represent a selection of the funniest and more unusual ambulance-call stories that have been collected from staff working in the London Ambulance Service.

One evening in mid winter an ambulance crew were called to take a man into hospital who had stopped breathing and, sadly, died. The body was taken to the mortuary which was just outside the casualty department and near the ambulance bay. The dead man was of the Jewish faith and a male relative asked if he could stay with the deceased overnight as it was their custom.

After some discussion this was agreed by the hospital. It was explained to the relative that it would be necessary to lock the perimeter gate to the mortuary for security reasons and to this he agreed.

Later, the night shift came on duty and were told about the man in the mortuary but unfortunately not all the staff were informed.

In the early hours of the morning, one of the porters went outside for a cigarette. It was very dark and cold and the only light was that in the ambulance bay.

Suddenly from behind him the porter heard a voice ....

"psst...excuse me."

The porter, slowly turning round saw a cold white face peering at him through the bars of the mortuary gates.

"Have you got another blanket? It's a bit cold in here."

THE FUNNY SIDE OF NURSING

The ambulance team was called to the doctors surgery to collect a female who had internal injuries after a fall. The crew were met by a doctor who was having difficulty concealing a smile. Before taking the crew in to see the patient, the doctor told them what had happened.

She said that the lady was at home doing the hoovering and as she was moving some furniture, she lost her balance and fell backwards onto the handle of the hoover, which entered her back passage.

As a precaution the doctor wanted the lady to go to hospital for an x-ray. The crew understand that the lady is now picking up nicely.

A crew were called to a house where an elderly man had collapsed. On arrival, the attendant was approached by the man's daughter, who explained that they had just attended her mother's funeral and that her father had taken it badly.

The driver, who was busy opening the back doors of the ambulance, heard nothing of this conversation.

Upon entering the house the driver met a large party of smartly dressed people, many with drinks in their hands. In another room he found the attendant chatting with the old man and explaining that they were taking him to the hospital for a check-up.

The driver, returning to the ambulance to collect the chair, was asked by various people in the house how the old man was. Being unaware of the situation he replied, "Don't worry, keep the party going, we'll soon have him back here joining in the knees-up."

THE FUNNY SIDE OF NURSING

A crew took an elderly male into hospital on the orders of his doctor. The patient was accompanied by his brother who was also elderly. While the crew were waiting to hand the patient over to the casualty staff, the patient suddenly remembered he had come out without his teeth. The patient's brother said, "No problem, I'll bring them up tomorrow."

"That's no good," said the patient, "I want them now."

Without further ado the brother took his own teeth out and gave them to his sickly brother who promptly popped them into his own mouth.

Looking to the two ambulance men the brother said, "Don't worry, we're always getting them mixed up anyway."

21

The location the crew were given was a well known lovers lane. The call was made by a female who sounded very distressed, so ambulance control also asked the police to attend. The crew arrived first and were waved down by the lady. She looked extremely embarrassed and led the crew to her car. There, they found a man kneeling in the back of the car in a state of undress. He was unable to move as his back had locked. Trying their best to maintain a professional air, the crew asked the lady how long he had been in that position. She told them about an hour, 45 minutes of which she had been pinned underneath him. She then asked the crew how long they would be as she was desperate to get home.

The crew explained that they had to wait for the police to arrive and at this the lady became furious, shouting,

"Why on earth did you have to call them?"

The crew assured her that she wasn't in any trouble but the lady replied...

"I will be when they arrive. My husband's a police officer."

Upon arrival at a call given simply as 'male fallen', the crew were met by members of the mans family in a particularly panicky state. The crew felt that the family were probably over reacting to the situation and determined to put them more at ease.

The attendant got out of the ambulance and went into the house with the family. The driver went round to the back of the ambulance and opened the doors, then he made his way into the house.

In an effort to cheer everyone up, the driver entered the house making the sound of a trumpet fanfare and calling out,

"Don't panic, the cavalry's arrived!"

He entered the room where everyone had gathered, to find all eyes staring at him in amazement. The old chap who had 'fallen' had in fact collapsed and died 45 minutes earlier.

An ill patient, in the back of an ambulance and on his way to hospital, kept saying to the attendant that he was sure he was going to die. The patient's wife and daughter, also in the ambulance, were obviously very upset.

In an attempt to reassure them, the attendant started saying that the man was OK and, as long as he did what the doctors told him and got plenty of rest, he would be fine.

For some reason the driver assumed that the attendant was talking about him so he turned on the ambulance intercom and said, "Don't believe a word he says, it's all lies!"

A crew were asked to call into the casualty department to collect an elderly man and take him home after treatment for a head injury. The Sister at casualty told the crew that the man was sitting in the waiting room. There they saw a man with a dressing over his eye and asked him if he was the man they were looking for. The man said he was, so the crew led him out to the ambulance and took him to the address they had been given.

Upon arrival the crew were met by an elderly lady who was delighted that her husband had been brought back. The crew led the man into the house and asked him where he wanted to go. The lady ushered him into the front room and sat him down. The crew explained to the lady that the man was probably still a little dazed from the accident and that a nice cup of tea and plenty of rest would work wonders. They then left.

About three hours later the Sister in casualty asked the crew why they hadn't taken the man home. They confirmed that they had but the Sister took them to the waiting room and pointed out the man she had meant.

The crew, completely bewildered, called through to control to tell them what had happened and were advised to take the second man home to the same address and try to find out who the first man was. On the journey there the second man said he was particularly worried about leaving his wife alone for so long as she was showing signs of dementia. At the house all three went to the door and let themselves in. The wife, who was pleased to see them told her husband that a friend of his had come to visit (obviously the first man) and they found him sitting comfortably, unperturbed, in the front room.

The man, also suffering from dementia, was unaware that anything was amiss and said that he had thoroughly enjoyed the afternoon.

Nurses notes...

Ensure the patient can eat himself.

Prior to a Barium Enema, the patient should have his rectum blown up.

Resuscitation:
1. Take pulse.
2. Ring Team.
3. Get them on the floor.
4. Resuss.

For example, the nurse might commence by encouraging the patient to ensure he is always wearing an acceptable trouser.

Highly medicated patients may be undesirable.

Trains were also a fascination for him. He enjoyed travelling in them and had, on one occasion in the past, travelled many hundreds of miles. This was a cause of great concern to his parents as he was just meant to be going down the road to collect his unemployment benefit.

(Referring to Sex Education)
This topic would always provide stimulation for some patients.

ECT can be described as a therapeutic dose of electricity to the ed.

Post a nurse to meet the daughter.

Hospital Notice...
Ambulance Service:- New roosters are being brought in by ambulance staff.

"Ambulance? Send new roosters...I'm completely worn out!"

He was asked not to eat or drink anything as this would help eliminate the problems of choking and inhaling.

After his bath, the patient was assisted into his gown with a nurse.

After his discharge, the patient did not push himself.

A sad point during his stay in hospital, was the death of his elderly cat. This was expected, but upset him, however it was interesting to note, that despite his death he was progressing well.

He would be approached each morning by the razor nurse to shave.

The Pharmacist talked at us instead of to us. He just kept throwing medicines at us.

The patient is a heavy smoker, but has been cut down by her doctor.

The nurse, together with the physiotherapist, will do active and passive exercises to prevent joint stiffness.

The TED stockings were removed for washing and replaced with a nurse.

THE FUNNY SIDE OF NURSING

On the wards...

A boy was just admitted to the hospital for a minor burn.
During the history he said,
"I have been in the hospital before."
"Why was that?" asked the nurse.
"I had to have my hemorrhoids removed."
"Hemorrhoids!" she said shaking her head, "Show me where
they were."
Gravely, the seven year old pointed down his throat.
"I was snoring so they took out my tonsils and hemorrhoids."

*Several years ago while working nights in a one room ICU, we
had an unusual night when all the patients were sleeping. We
decided to get some practice time with the 'Rescusi-Annie'
dummy. We hauled her up from the practice lab in her
suitcase, unpacked her and laid her in an empty bed. We all
took turns giving her mouth to mouth. When we'd finished, we
packed her in the suitcase and returned her to the practice lab.
The next morning the lady in the bed across from where we
were practicing motioned the doctor close and whispered,
"Get me out of here! Last night the lady in that bed died and
when they couldn't revive her they packed her in a suitcase!"*

A new nurse came to our ward. When one of the doctors came
to do the rounds she was the only nurse available at the time to
go with him. During his rounds, a patient complained about
having difficulty sitting because of perineal discomfort. The
doctor told the new nurse to get the patient a donut. The nurse
promptly went to the 'phone and made a call. After the call
she returned to the room to tell the doctor and the patient, "The
kitchen is out of donuts, but will apple pie do?"

The new auxiliary reported to the staff nurse that one of the patients had had a good result from the suppositories administered earlier. "Put it in the bowel book," she was told. The next person to open the book got a very unpleasant surprise.

The new training for nurses, introduced in the mid 1980's, caused a lot of problems on the wards; students, formerly part of the work force, were now only allowed to come on the wards and watch what was going on.
One such student was looking at the 'off duty' list, a puzzling grid full of strange letters and abbreviations. Most of them he could work out: DO: day off; SN: staff nurse, and so on.
But right at the bottom, before his own surname, was the acronym JAFO. He struggled with it: junior associate.. junior allocation... In the end, he asked a passing auxiliary.
"Easy Luv'," she said, "just another f***ing observer."

The following occurred recently outside the main entrance of a famous London teaching hospital:
A young man was handing out leaflets inviting passers-by to Evensong and Sunday mass at a nearby church, with many "Praise the Lords" and "Hallelujahs" thrown in.
Two nurses emerged from the building, looking tired and fed up after what has obviously been a long shift.
They politely took the proffered leaflet but when the young man told them: "Rejoice - Jesus saves" the older of the two was heard to mutter loudly: "He wouldn't if he got my salary!"

Mrs X, an elderly patient on a medical ward, told the student nurse that she desperately wanted to use the toilet. Overhearing this as she passed, the ward sister said: "Don't forget, nurse, this lady is on strict bed rest."
A few minutes later, Sister was passing through the ward again, and was horrified to see the patient's head waving to and fro above the curtains around her bed. She hurried to investigate, and found the lady sitting on a commode, balanced precariously on her bed.

As soon as possible following appointment, usually during the first week, all nurses will attend an Induction Curse.

Sexually uninhibited behaviour would be included in the plan of care.

Night staff will assess the patient's ability with a bottle in bed.

If the patient is unable or unwilling to eat himself, a nurse should help him do so.

She will be weighed twice weekly on Monday morning (by night staff wearing underclothes only).

Encourage him to eat at mealtimes, if he doesn't, supplement his diet with smacks.

Anxiety can cause many physical symptoms, e.g. hair standing upright on neck and shoulders.

The nurse would observe the patient's trousers for any abnormal swellings.

If a lot of doctors go around the patient's barrier-nursing bed, then there would be speculation.

The future for him is poor at present. Progress would be better if mother gave up depression or if father behaves himself.

(Referring to Behaviour Modification programme)
'The patient could be flooded'.

She, and her husband if necessary, should be told that a hysterectomy doesn't curtail sexual activities. Just because the 'cradle' has been removed doesn't mean the 'play-pen' isn't still intact.

Hopefully, get decent client clothing, i.e. not half-mast trousers. Integration is the key word, not allowing it to stick out like a sore thumb.

Is there a possibility of anorexia nervosa? Everything must be weighed-up.

Never should a nurse come up to a patient and handle him, without the first, reassuring touch.

The nurse must bear in mind that people belong to a variety of different religions such as Muslims, Jews and Genitals.

Life in the middle ages was not a bowel of cherries.

The anaesthetic will dry up all body secretions and the patient may become a prune if an IVI is not put up.

You can best describe pressure area care as, turn, turn, turn, turn, turn, turn, and turn again.

When the man dies, the wife must not be brushed under the carpet.

Breathing is essential if the patient is to mobilise correctly.

The laundry of an infected patient should be double bagged with the nurse.

I felt that the session on 'Differences Between the Sexes' was OK, as a slot-in subject.

There was a lack of apathy from patients towards detoxification and withdrawal.

For most of the day he had been wandering around on his own, occasionally attaching himself to a member of staff.

Shortly after (admission) he caught chicken pox. He went to a side-room in the main hospital, complete with television, tape recorder and a nurse from the Unit.

She met an older, married man and they had an affair, but he left her for his wife.

I calmed her down by calling her names quietly.

Positive reinforcement was given, such as warm smiles and praise when Mr Martin sits on the toilet.

Primary nurse will spend at least half a house each day talking to the patient.

Some patients who have a mastectomy get quite upset, while others just laugh it off.

Whilst she was being laid on the floor...

THE FUNNY SIDE OF NURSING

When I was a student nurse, a story was told about one of my classmates who went to get her patient ready for physical therapy. He had just had a stroke and was not much help with the transfer. She had finally gotten him into a sitting position and was about to call for assistance when the doctor came into the room. The MD asked what she was doing. She said that she was getting the patient up for physical therapy.
"That's strange" said the doctor, "I was coming in to sign the death certificate."

In the week prior to the Grand National horse race, I decided to organise a "sweep" on a particular ward with some quite poorly, terminally ill patients in an attempt to normalise their situation and provide some light hearted entertainment.

I cut out the names of the horses from the local newspaper and put them into a receiver and asked one of the student nurses to give the staff and patients the opportunity to pick a horse at random.

Time passed and on her return to the office she had a somewhat perplexed look on her face when I asked her if all the horses had been chosen, along with the completed list of owners. She said that all the horses and owners were accounted for apart from Mr X's, and she was unable to tell which horse he had chosen as he had eaten his!

Apparently, this very trusting man, having been offered the receiver, thought it contained a tablet and promptly put the little ball of newspaper into his mouth and swallowed, much to the student nurse's horror.

We later identified his horse through a process or elimination and he in fact won the race!

THE FUNNY SIDE OF NURSING

The patient was placed on a fluid balance chart.

The patient, who is to have a Thyroidectomy, may have fears about her head coming off.

Some women experience mood swings after this operation, but she told me she was so relieved to be rid of the cause of these long standing problems, that she didn't really feel inclined to have mood swings.

He was affected in both knees, although his right knee had been fine since he had both his hands and elbows replaced.

He weighed 72kgs which was a satisfactory weight for his weight.

Of course some patients who come into hospital do die. This can be a very tense time for the patient.

As far as nursing the elderly is concerned, nurses have a major disadvantage, in that they are human.

(Evaluation of an 'Aggression Workshop')
"I thought this was useful... taught me some methods I might use if faced with violet attacks."

The Nursing Officer was appalled by the cleanliness of the ward.

The Anaesthetist contrived to inflate my patient until he started to breath again.

Patients seeking advice on welfare rights should attend the Welfare Rights clinic which is hell every Tuesday from 10:00am to 11:00am.

The patient had had problems with his sight for several days and the doctor thought this was probably due to a detached rectum.

Assistance will need to be given by the nurse with hygiene needs.

The environment should be calm and quiet as possible to calm the frayed nerves, but not so calm that the over all effect is pure boredom, some sort of stimulus is needed.

An hourly observation of blood pressure must be recorded every half hour.

You empty the catheter by using a pair of gloves.

To define stress, you will have to have suffered from it at least once in a life time, which I am sure you will already have. You worry about such things as money, meals, sleep, interblock work etc. unnecessarily. You may not sleep at night, your body uncontrollably twitching and panic setting in at any minute.

Poor appetite and weight loss, also reduces body weight.

Very often the patient's bladder will object to the catheter.

Patience and more patience cannot be stressed enough when dealing with patients.

With the reproductive system, especially in woman, the menopause occurs. This is when the female is no longer able to produce young, as they stop menstruating. This does not however happen in the mail.

The nurse must stick to the patient's bedtime.

Tepid sponging can take place by splitting the body into three parts, face, trunk and lower limbs.

Exam Question: Why do prescription drugs vary from over-the-counter drugs?
Answer: Some drugs have a more lusting effect.

It would be unsafe at this stage to examine the current practice for administering ECT.

The nurse should regularly introduce herself by name to give him more chance to become familiar with her.

She stated that she had not had sexual relations with him for some time, due to his phobia about mice.

Locked Door Policy:- (Nursing Officer) was concerned about the knob: felt it was too small.

The exhibition held alongside the RCN congress was extremely well attended, not least because there were any number of interesting freebies on offer. Sample tubes of a (very expensive) calendula-based gel (marketed as an antenatal aid to prevent stretch marks) seemed particularly desirable to one nurse, who returned to its manufacturer's stand no fewer than 14 times to pick up a handful. Finally the salesperson running the stand could not resist asking her if she would be recommending the gel to her clients.

"No," came the reply, "I am an EN in an old people's home."

"So have you found that our gel is also good for older skin?" asked the salesperson, sensing perhaps another marketing angle in the offing.

"No," said the enrolled nurse, "but it buffs up my mahogany furniture a treat."

Overheard in the A & E department of a West London hospital: A young man, slightly the worse for wear, is called by the triage nurse to assess his problem. Through the open door of the triage room the other assembled Saturday night casualties cannot help overhearing him telling the nurse that he has fallen over the pool-table in a pub and now his leg is 'giving him gyp'.

"It's my right leg, the one that I've broken twice before," he whines.

"Once I fell out of a tree and bust it, and the second time I did it in while I was slam-dancing."

"Old trouble with the fibula," the nurse murmurs while writing on his admission card, only to be interrupted with an outraged yell of "Oi, hold on, I'm telling you the God's honest truth!"

After a blow-out Christmas dinner on the elderly care ward, the patients were all settled in front of the Queen's speech on TV, and the charge nurse called his staff in for a sherry in his office - all except the student nurse, who was left to keep an eye on things. "You could collect in their teeth and give them a good scrub, if you're worried about getting bored," she was told.

Half an hour later, the staff returned, to find the student crying miserably, while the patients all seemed to be leering and grinning horribly. "What on earth's going on here?" the charge nurse demanded.

In between sobs, the story came out. The student had filled a large bowl with Steradent and hot water, and then collected all the teeth in, but was having trouble matching them up with their original owners.

One day while weighing a little old man in our nursing home...
"Good morning, Mr Abercrombie," I said. "It's time to get weighed."
He looked up at me in an odd way with a sudden sparkle in his eyes.
"I'll say it's time," he said, "I haven't been laid in years!"

An elderly woman on the orthopeadic floor (who was hard of hearing) was to have a phlebotomy due to her polycythemia. After the physician discussed the procedure with her, I proceeded to set up the equipment.
When I gave the patient the permit form to sign, she asked several questions.
"Wouldn't this hurt a great deal?", "Are they going to do it right here?" and, "Are *you* going to do it?"
After further probing on my part, the patient broke out into a giggle and exclaimed, "Oh, I thought you said you were going to do a lobotomy!"

A retired nurse in her 70's was a patient in the ICU. She was alert but a bit disorientated after her surgery. In a nearby cubicle, a confused elderly male patient was having difficulty settling down, even though he was attended to appropriately. When he was left alone he would shout out "Nurse! Nurse!" relentlessly. At one point, his neighbour, the retired nurse, shouted back from her bed, "I'm busy right now, but I'll be there in a minute."

Examination papers...

Question: From what may men in their fifties suffer?
Answer: The manopause.

Question: What is a common treatment for a badly bleeding nose?
Answer: Circumcision.

Question: How should nurses prepare a patient before a pre-med injection?
Answer: They must wash a patient's groin and genial areas.

Question: How can parents help when a child wakes in the night suffering from breathing difficulties?
Answer: Make them inhale a steam kettle.

"You mean you're not getting in?"

The patient should be sat upright in bed between two nurses.

The patient's limbs should be below his waist.

If resuscitation fails and the patient dies, I would ensure that she was placed in a side-room so that no one on the ward could find her.

To prevent infection, all you need is common sense. If in doubt, double check your doubts and this will bring infection down to a minimum, which is where it should be.

The pyrexial patient would not wear makeup if she is expiring.

To prevent pressure sores, the nurse can spread the weight of the patient as often as possible.

THE FUNNY SIDE OF NURSING

We were all somewhat startled at the nurses' station when one of our female patients called out for someone to bring her the urinal. We looked at each other, a bit bewildered. Did we hear that right?
Then the ward clerk realized this Swedish lady was asking for the morning newspaper, the 'Yournal.'

A nurse described how she was in the emergency department, with an alcoholic man who was going through D.T.'s. Trying to get a vein for an IV, she started patting his forearm.
The patient said, "Yeah, Luv, I see them too." and started swatting at his arm with her.

Whilst working as a District Nursing Sister, I was asked by the GP to visit an elderly patient to administer two suppositories to relieve constipation. Unbeknown to me, I had been given the wrong address. Arriving on the doorstep, I was welcomed to enter and though a little surprised, the gentleman was glad to see me and said his wife was in bed upstairs. The GP had visited earlier and told her to rest. The wife unfortunately was very deaf and just kept nodding whilst I asked the relevant questions.
My task completed, I left and arranged a follow-up visit. Later, on arriving back at the Health Centre, there was a message waiting for me asking why I hadn't been able to visit the constipated lady?

As a first year student I was on my second placement, a medical ward. After supper I asked the Staff Nurse to help me turn a male patient who had suffered a stroke and was unconscious. As we walked towards his bed the Staff Nurse said she was going to get in touch with his relatives. I went to the bedside and started talking to him, giving him eye and mouth care whilst explaining to him that we were about to change his position. Although unconscious, I had been told that hearing is the last sense to go. Ten minutes later the Staff Nurse returned and told me I could pull the sheet over him. It was only then I realised that for ten minutes I had been talking to a dead man!

"Here, feel this, tell me what you think."

While working in an Emergency Assessment Clinic at a psychiatric hospital, a common question asked during assessment of clients is - "Do you have a criminal record?" One evening the doctor who was new to psychiatry, asked - "Do you have a Police record?" The client replied "Yes." The doctor then asked if he could elaborate. The client replied, "I've got Every Breath You Take and Walking On The Moon." The doctor did not understand why the nursing staff present were unable to contain their laughter!

As a student nurse I attended a lecture on rigor mortis. It was explained to us that as the process evolves the tips of the fingers and lips turn blue and the penis stiffens. The lecturer went on to discuss many other aspects of death and dying.
At the end of the session, we were asked if there were any questions. A male colleague asked the very 'prim and proper' female lecturer if she would explain the process of rigor mortis once again. She duly did as requested, finishing with the statement that the penis stiffens. She asked if he had any further questions.
"Yes," he replied, "Can you put your hand in my pocket, I think I'm dying!"
The class erupted with laughter as the red-faced lecturer stormed from the room.

Whilst visiting an elderly gentleman following his discharge from hospital, after a trans-urethral Prostatectomy he said, "You seem to know a lot about this operation young lady, have you had it done?"

Problem:- The patient may experience a lack of libido leading to anxiety.
Nursing Care:- A nurse should explain that this is due to his illness, and it will lift once he improves.

The patient's elimination should be measured and recorded.

The patient should be de-lavatated.

Put head back, hold patient's nose and give five blows in the mouth.

This being the case, the nurses would play skittles or ball with the gentlemen.

The patient needs to wash her own clothes to last a full wee.

He could be referred to Alcoholics Anonymost.

Woman clients may not like the men being there, interfering with them.

Medication, where necessary, should be taken by the qualified nurse. (Referring to a day-trip)

He needs to develop confidence, be assertive and show his assets.

The blood should be ordered to come up to the ward, the nurse must give the porter the slip before he disappears.

THE FUNNY SIDE OF NURSING

More ambulance stories...

A drunken male was making his way home across a park. Due to his condition he stumbled and fell, cutting his eye. It was raining and when the ambulance crew arrived, the man was covered in mud, blood and grass.

The crew helped the man into the ambulance and started to clean him up in order to have a proper look at his cut. Whilst cleaning his face, one of the crew saw what looked like a small lump of mud on his nose, so he pulled this off with his fingernails. The man, who had been no trouble at all so far, suddenly jumped up shouting and swearing.

Unknown to the crew, the man had fallen a few days earlier and cut his nose which had required stitches. The ambulance man had promptly removed the scab and pulled out the stitches.

Some eagle-eyed bystander who was at a road traffic accident, noticed that part of the ambulance's number plate read DOA. The bystander felt that the number plate was inappropriate and wrote in to complain.

The number was swiftly changed. In medical terms DOA means Dead on Arrival.

52

Ambulance call...
'Bang, bang, whoosh, whoosh...please investigate..'
On arrival the crew were met by a foreign gentleman who was obviously very happy to see them.
The man could speak little English, but beckoned the crew into the house and led them to the central heating boiler.
The crew, both looking confused, asked the man how they could help. The man banged the boiler twice and said, "Bang, bang, whoosh, whoosh, no good."
The crew rang the gas board for him.

At the scene of the accident the ambulance crew found four police officers holding down a seemingly aggressive young man. The man had suffered a bad head injury, was behaving violently and was an obvious danger to himself.

While the police were holding him down the crew examined him. They found two scalp wounds and, because of the way he was acting, a fractured skull was suspected.

With great difficulty the crew, with the help of the police, managed to get the man into the ambulance and off to hospital. There, the major trauma room had been prepared with doctors and nurses ready and waiting.

Upon arrival, the man was still thrashing around and totally unaware of what was happening. Again, with the help of the police, the crew successfully transferred the patient onto a hospital trolley and into the trauma room. Everybody continued to restrain the man so that the doctors could have a good look at him.

The man, still struggling, managed to break free of one of his arm grips and grabbed the first thing he could get hold of. Unfortunately this was an ambulance man's testicles!

The crew member, screaming, desperately tried to back away with the injured man, refusing to let go, being wheeled about the room with an entourage of police and medical staff in tow. More help was soon at hand, the mans grip was eventually loosened and we understand that both men have now made full recoveries.

An ambulance crew arrived at a house and were met by a man who was holding his throat and looking very distressed. The man managed to tell the crew that he had swallowed some bleach. The crew heard a woman crying from another room and discovered the man's wife in a state of shock, her face covered in blood. The man explained what had happened.

His wife had used an empty mouth wash bottle to store some bleach, but hadn't told him about it. He had taken a gulp from the bottle (which she had left in the bathroom) and immediately spat it out. His mouth started to burn and he started coughing. His wife came running into the bathroom to see what all the noise was about. She was trying to help him, but at the same time, found it amusing.

The man, with his head in the toilet, didn't see the humour and reacted by swinging out, punching her in the face, causing her nose to bleed. Both were taken to hospital.

As a second year student I was working on an all male psychiatric ward. Unfortunately, one of our longstanding in-patients had just died and I noticed that he hadn't got his teeth in. I looked in his locker but to no avail so I asked the charge nurse, who told me to look in the sluice room.

There I found a white denture pot with a set of false teeth in so I proceeded to try to fix them into the dead man's mouth (before he froze!).

I had been trying for about a minute when I overheard a patient asking another nurse where his false teeth had gone. I suddenly realised whose teeth I had!

Panicking slightly, I quickly put them back into their container and took them to the patient saying I had been to clean them. He promptly put them in without the knowledge that they had just been sitting in the mouth of a dead man.

On the way to theatre, the nurse should try to re-insure the patient.

The nurse must give the patient a sputum pot, noting the colour and consistency of it.

Primary Nursing may not suit all staff, as some like to muddle along behind a screen of confusion and management, rather than be accountable for their actions.

When a woman has the menopause, her periods don't just suddenly stop, but they trickle out.

Nursing staff should maintain a safe environment by avoiding contact with certain fellow patients.

His sexual advances could be very distressing to female patients and female staff. The staff may insist on a male member on duty at all times.

(Notes made by nurse preparing for a rehabilitation class)
...I would start off with a session on alcohol abuse.

When the patient proclaims, "Bless you my child. All your sins are forgiven" the nurse should respond by saying something like; "You're not the Messiah. Come and help me make the beds."

Foot or finger tapping can be an indication of impending aggression, as will dilated pupils and teeth gringing.

It is always advantageous to gain inexperience in aggression management.

They were denied many social skills such as using their hands to eat at mealtimes instead of cutlery.

THE FUNNY SIDE OF NURSING

Doctors notes...

She slipped on ice and apparently her legs went in separate directions in early December.

Patient was seen in consultation with another doctor, who felt she should sit tight on the abdomen. I agreed.

Sister Anna Maria is a Catholic nun who is currently in between missionaries.

The patient was found to have 12 children by her doctor.

The patient has been depressed ever since she started seeing me.

The review team was pleased to note that movement among learners was minimal, and only happened as a last resort.

Nurses notes...

If the time and effort can be made then it should be. I would be neglecting my duties as a nurse if I did not.

The nurse should use the orthodox method when lifting up the bed.

Physiotherapy is given to stop sputum clogging up the lungs.

Deep breathing should be done to prevent a DVT.

The breathless patient should be nursed in the opthalmic position.

If only a small branch of the heart is blocked, the region of the heart muscle supplied by it becomes neurotic and dead.

Reasons for catheterisation:
  a) Before or after pregnancy
  b) Before or after surgery

A trip by the barber may enhance the patient's looks.

Encourage communication by getting him to sit next door to another patient.

The Operating Theatre assessment can be an eye opener for the nurse.

In old age, blood vessels become thin and electric.

The nurse herself can prevent cross infection, by good standards of hand washing after handling contaminated diet, like bedpans.

Weil's disease is carried by rats excreted in urine.

In her previous life she experienced no problems.

(Referring to signs of aggression)
...loss of eye contact, frowning and clenching of lists.

Give the patient time to eat, do not push him.

SCRATCH

BONX

Pete williams

The patients themselves might start an infection, by being inquisitive and having a peep under a sterile dressing and using their fingers which may have earlier been used for turning the pages of a dirty book.

Samuel Tuke was one of the famous Quackers.

During sleep the body gets to work repairing and maintaining any damaged tissue and frightening any infection.

Emergency Arrest:
1. Lay patient out on a firm surface head back. Remove obstructions to the mouth.
2. Put fingers on pulse bang sternum.
3. One bang on chest check pulse.
4. One blow in the mouth five on chest.

THE FUNNY SIDE OF NURSING

It was an extremely busy morning on the medical ward and the nurse apologised profusely when she finally reached the old gentleman waiting for a wash.
"I'm afraid we've only got time for a catlick today," she explained, and to her surprise the man became very agitated. "How dare you!" he shouted, "I'm a Protestant!"

THIS
SIDE
EVEN
DATES

A word about
COMIC RELIEF

Charity Projects was established in 1984 to help disadvantaged people in Africa and the UK realise their aspirations and potential. It all began with an Arts Festival in Nether Wallop, and developed through a series of events until 1986, when the Young Ones and Cliff Richard stormed the charts with their melodious version of "Livin' Doll". Comic Relief was born, to be followed 2 years later by its riotous sibling, the red nose.

The intention of that first Red Nose Day, and those that have followed was to combine two time-honoured characteristics of the British - generosity, and the potential for *extreme* eccentricity! As we succumbed to the power of the red nose, inhibitions were recklessly cast aside - for one day people would do anything if you sponsored them! Nationwide we surrendered to urges to bathe in baked beans, or walk in jelly-filled wellies - putting the "fun" back into "fundraising". After a day of fantastically lucrative lunacy, everyone was rewarded with a night of TV on BBC1. Rib-splitting comedy and powerful documentaries combined to keep the nation transfixed, and donations flooded in. By the evening's end £15 million had been raised, and an institution born. "Charity" would never be quite the same...

Since then Comic Relief hasn't looked back. Every other year (since going bi-annual in 1989) organisations and enterprising individuals have thought up increasingly ridiculous ways to fundraise. The total so far is over £112 million, of which every penny has been allocated to projects. Of the money raised, two thirds goes towards long-term development in Africa, and one third remains in the UK, helping both older people, and young people who are homeless, disabled or who have problems with drugs or alcohol.

Also available...

A truly hilarious collection of anecdotes, misprints, misquotes and exam howlers from Britain's classrooms. With a donation of 10% to **COMIC RELIEF** from every copy sold.

Rural Science exam question: What steps would you take to eliminate garden pests?
Answer: The steps I would take would be very heavy ones.

Question: How important are elections to a democratic world?
Answer: Sex can only happen when a male gets an election.

Price £4.99
ISBN 0 9526395 0 5

This title, first published in 1995, can still be ordered from all good book shops if not currently in stock.

Acknowledgements

Special thanks are made to the following:

Contributors

Brian Booth, M. Burton, Gail Cox, Hazel Elliott, Marion Evans, Margaret Ford, Robert Garbett, Carolyn Gibbon, Dave Glanvill (ambulance stories), Jean Gray, V.A. Hodgson, Rob Johnstone, Mike Jones, Ronata Langford, Mike Lehane, Julie Lovegrove, Paul Mangan, Ruth Marshall, Nigel Northcott, Steve Riches from *Yes* Magazine, Graham Scott, Mary Shek, Shirley Slipman, Marie Thomason, Steve Wittberger. Thanks also for the help and co-operation of the staff and readers of *Nursing Standard* and *Nursing Times*.

Cartoonists

Quentin Blake, Paul Cemmick, Allan Davies, Pete Dredge, Noel Ford, Martin Honeysett, Larry, Fran Orford, Ken Pyne, Max Steiger, Colin Taylor, Nigel Thomas, Geoff Thompson, Pete Williams.

Cover photograph taken from *'The A-Z of Behaving Badly'* and reproduced with the kind permission of Pavilion Books Ltd.

Cover illustration by John Richardson, Richardson Studios, Cleveland Lodge, 45 Cleveland Terrace, Darlington DL3 7HD.